COME UNTO ME

MATTHEW 11:28

MARIETA   MILLER-COLLINS

Order this book online at www.trafford.com
or email orders@trafford.com

Most Trafford titles are also available at major online book retailers.

All Scriptures quotations from The King James Bible

Song Lyrics from "Why am I still Here" and "You Can't Hide" by Russ and
Louise McMillion of Latter Rain Ministries, used by permission.

Printed in the United States of America.

ISBN: 978-1-4669-5155-6 (sc)
ISBN: 978-1-4669-5154-9 (e)

Trafford rev. 09/19/2012

Trafford
PUBLISHING® www.trafford.com

North America & international
toll-free: 1 888 232 4444 (USA & Canada)
phone: 250 383 6864 ♦ fax: 812 355 4082

Contents

✠ ✠ ✠

This Book has been written in obedience to the one true God.

It may be well with us, when we obey the voice of the Lord our God.

Jeremiah 42:6

God has given me a recurring vision, which comforts and blesses me in times of trial. Jesus is standing with His arms outstretched to me. He is smiling, and say's, "Come unto me!" Thus the title of this book.

Come unto me, all ye that labor and are heavy laden, and I will give you rest.

Matthew 11:28

✠ ✠ ✠

Dedication

Thanks, from my heart, to my Granddaughter, Caitlin Jordan, a sophomore, at Columbus College of Art and Design, Columbus, Ohio, for doing the cover illustration. Great job! I love you!

Grandma

This book is dedicated to all my family that said "Do it!" Thanks for the encouragement and help. You are my heart. I love you.

Mom and Grandma

To my life long cheer leaders, my (sissy) Merlena Parish, and to my (Cousin, Sister) Judy Ruble. I know you've always got my back, and I will always have yours.

Love you, Love you, Reety
God Bless you.

✠ ✠ ✠

Introduction

July 7, 1995, I had a dream I was planting flower seeds in front of a tall brick building resembling an apartment house. When a man dressed in a white robe walked up beside me and asked what I was doing.

I said, "I was planting flower seeds"

He smiled and softly replied, "No, you're sowing the word"

March 4, 1999, I had a dream I was sitting on a bench in a garden when a man carrying a Bible walked over to me. He looked at the book lying beside me. He said he was a preacher and noticed the book lying on the bench and wondered if he could read it. I said, No, it was just a book of my memories and I didn't want anyone to read it.

He said "Oh, Okay then."

He turned and walked away leaving me sitting alone with a closed book of memories. I laid my hand on top of the book, and watched him walk away.

I believe God was telling me in the first dream He was going to use me by sowing his word.

In the second dream I believe I am to share all the love God has shown me over the years. That is what this book is about, Memories!

✠ ✠ ✠

Testimonials

"I have known Marieta Collins for about 15 years and can attest to these facts concerning her walk with the Lord, Jesus Christ.

Marieta has consistently exhibited all the qualities that a church needs to attract new members and to enhance church growth. She has always been one of those who are among the first to greet visitors and to make them feel both needed and appreciated.

She is accustomed to and expects God to perform miracles because she has found the "secret" to attaining all God's promises and that "secret" is simply just to expect Him to do what He said He would do.

If I was not a full time Evangelist, and again became a pastor, this is the kind of folks that I would hope God would send me to shepherd. I highly recommend her in any Christian setting and sincerely believe that she would be an asset to any church body."

Evangelist's Russell and Louise McMillion
Latter Rain Ministries
www.latterrainministires.com

✠ ✠ ✠

"It has been over 30 years since High School that I had seen Doug. That previous weekend I had been in Michigan visiting churches, and had asked the Lord to let me see Doug in the yard. As in past time I would look for him hoping to see him again after all of these years. Actually, I went by the house and caught a glimpse of two men in the yard and decided to turn around and go back to the Collin's house. It was Doug and his dad finishing up evening chores.

Doug invited me into his home and he introduced me to his wife Marieta. I thought it odd that she would ask "Why did you stop here today?" Of course, it was "ordered of the Lord."

Since knowing her, Marieta has been a great blessing to House of Prayer in Kenton, Ohio"

Doug Copp
Carltonville, South Africa

✠ ✠ ✠

"My wife Shirley and I met Marieta Collins in 1992. Having been in the ministry for 50 years, our observation of Marieta portrays the life that we always desire in our converts.

First and most important is her love for the Lord. She not only talks about it, she lives it. Her love for God is evident in her life. Even in trying times she is a beautiful example of that love. Maybe the words we should use are, "Steadfast and reliable"

Her heart and soul is to spread the gospel, not only to see her family and friends saved. I'm sure this is her continual prayer. To correct the above statement, she desires all she comes in contact with, either by person or the word of a friend, to be saved.

At present she is teaching the adult study class at the church where we attend. The House of Prayer. Not only is she always prepared by study and prayer, but most important she allows the Spirit to lead and move through her.

We have not read this book, but we are anxious to see it in print, because we know it is true.

Paul and Shirley Ramsey

✠ ✠ ✠

Mrs. Marieta Collins is a devout Christian. A Holy Ghost filled believer who teaches our Adult Sunday School class. At the House of Prayer Pentecostal Church of God, 503 Summit St. Kenton, Ohio, 43326.

Marieta is a sincere, dedicated and anointed woman of God. We believe you will be blessed and encouraged in reading this book. Sister Marieta has been faithful and has been such a blessing. My wife Ruth and I believe that this book will encourage and touch many lives. We also believe souls will be saved. We are proud to be Marieta's Pastors.

Pastors Don & Ruth Holbrook

✠ ✠ ✠

Acknowledgment

It took a total of twelve years from the night God told me He would use me, to the completion of this book. God had to show me He was in control, and I had to give him my obedience. It wasn't that I didn't want to obey him, I did, and I just had no confidence in myself. I let the devil beat me down in that area of my life. Until God told me to do it afraid, and to be bold and step out. When I did God really started the wheels to turning. Everything started to fall into place, one after the other.

God first furnished the money from an unexpected source. Just as I had asked," In his time and in his way, and that I ask no man for a penny." When God's hand is in something, hold on, because you are going to be excited to see how He brings things together.

There were times in the two months it began, from money to publisher, that some negativity was spoken, but I refused to listen to it. This is God's book! I know God said to write it, and I knew God would remove any stumbling block that came along and get this book published. The biggest stumbling block crumbled when I did as God told me too, and "I stepped out in the boldness."

God knows whose hands He wants this book put into, I don't. I do know He gave me the honor of being the servant He chose to use. I humbly "Thank you Father."

My thanks also goes to the following people.

My granddaughter, Caitlin Jordan, for designing the book cover, My Great niece Hayley Gray who did the typing of the manuscript by Microsoft word file for me. My daughter Christy Beery, and her daughter, my Granddaughter Shelby Collins worked together sending, receiving and getting me the email from Doug Copp in South Africa. To Pastor Don and Ruth Holbrook, and our church secretary, Sally Motter for locating Brother Copp's email address. To Brother Russ and Sister Louise McMillion, for permission to use their song lyrics, and their kind words. Brother Doug Copp, Brother Paul and Sister Shirley Ramsey, My Pastors Don & Sister Ruth Holbrook, for the kind words and encouragement. My Brothers and Sisters of the House of Prayer, for always standing in prayer with me and for me when needed. I love you. God Bless you all.

Finally, to Carol Livingston, for the kindness she showed me. Thank you for being that door. God Bless.

I have so many more testimonies, of the past, the present and I know in the future. God isn't finished with me yet!

✠ ✠ ✠

Chapter 1

When Are You Going To Obey Me?

In the fall of 2004, Evangelist's Russ and Louise McMillion of Latter Rain Ministries gave me a tape they had just recorded, titled "In His Eyes". As soon as the song "Why Am I Still Here" began to play I heard the Lord plainly say to me "I have a message for you on this tape, Listen for it!" I heard Louise sing, "**But I know that I must stay to help Light the way for the one who would come to You.**" I heard God say, "Write my book, when are you going to obey Me?" I said "Lord, I want to obey you, but God why would you choose me to write a book for you?"

Russ went on to say **"It's really not mine to question. I am that I am, child be still!"** I had no doubt God was speaking to me with love and authority. I turned the tape over and my message continued as if there had been no pause in conversation from the last song on side one, to the first song on side two. Coincidence? Not hardly, this is how God works.

Russ began to speak again, **"I need to tell you today if there is a calling upon your life, say yes to the master. Just go to Him with open arms and say, "Yes, Lord I'm willing to do that thing** that you've called me to do." And if he's called you child he's already equipped you."

God really used the song, "You Cant Hide" to speak to me. I said "Okay, Lord"; I'm ready to obey you. Show me how to get published. I want you to furnish the money I don't want any doubt from anyone this book is from you. I will ask no one for a penny. I put all the details in your hands Lord. I want everything done your way and in your time. This is your book."

The Lord then told me, "You are not the only one I have called to write a book, I have called others. Each book will be different yet the same. You are to write a book of short stories of the blessings you have received from me, the miracles you have received, the visitations and visions you have received and the healings of which are many. Write this book because I have children that are babes yet and will need encouragement, and knowledge that I love them and I will never leave or forsake them. I will always walk beside them through any trial just as I have you."

Years ago, I ask God to use me in any way he chose, large or small. I don't care how. Now he is. I thank him for the honor.

Blessed be God, even the Father of our Lord Jesus Christ, the Father of mercies, and the God of all comfort: Who comforted us in all our tribulations, that we may be able to comfort them which are in any trouble, by the comfort where with we ourselves are comforted by God.

2 Corinthians 1:3-4

✠ ✠ ✠

Chapter 2

The Door Is Opened

In 2000, during one of my late night talks with Jesus, the Lord told me "He was going to give me a ministry." I laughed and said. "Lord, I'm 51 years old; I'm too old to start a ministry." God answered me back by saying, "Moses was 80 years old when I began using him. I can use you at any age." I asked what kind of ministry he was going to give me. God told me it would be of His choosing, and in His time, not mine. That was fine with me; if my ministry is not from God then there will be no anointing upon it. You just can't win souls for Christ without His anointing, and I want to be a soul winner.

In 2002, God told me He wanted me to write a book, and what was to be in it. I began going through all my journals I had kept since the seventies. All the trials, valleys, heartaches and the victories Jesus brought me through. The sweet conversations, and visitations I was blessed with, the many times He strengthened me. This child slips a lot it seems, but God is always there to catch me before I hit the ground. God is always patient, comforting, and forgiving no matter what I do. It just takes one word from Jesus to put my feet back on the right path.

I had asked God to use me, now He was going to. The bible says in Matthew 7:7, **Ask and it shall be given you, seek, and ye shall find; knock, and it shall be opened to you.**

I ask and the door was opened a couple years later. On the twenty-seventh day of November, 2004, I was reading the newspaper, and on the front page was a picture of a lady holding a book. My heart jumped. Above her picture was written "Forest author hopes her book will help readers through tough times." I heard the Lord say so plainly, "There you go!" My eyes were darting from the heading to the picture. I took a deep breath and began to read the article.

The authors name was Carol Linvingston. She kept a box of notes, I keep journals, God helped her through trials, He helps me, this book was her mission from God, a ministry and my book is my ministry from God. I knew deep inside this was no coincidence. I knew Carol was my door. God did what He said He would do, He opened a door. Now I had to walk through it.

I cut the article out, and prayed about what to do next. The Lord told me to write to Carol and tell her I was writing a book. I was to ask if she would give me advice on getting it published. I told the Lord I was afraid if I wrote a letter to Carol she might think I was some kind of a nut case. I did not hear from God for a couple of days. I felt in my spirit He was going to do something to let me know He was in control, not me.

I was watching Joyce Meyer on TV and all of a sudden I heard her say, "Do it afraid" I knew God was speaking to me again. I felt his Love and His smile. I laughed and said, "Okay Lord, you got me, you opened the door, now I'm going to walk through it. I am sure this is from you, I'll do it afraid, and I'll do it because I know you are with me."

I wrote to Carol on the 30th explaining everything to her. As I put her letter in the mailbox I prayed, asking the Holy Spirit to please anoint my words so when Carol reads them she would believe God was using her to help me obey Him.

On December 8th at 7:15 pm. I received a phone call from Carol. This was another confirmation from God to write a book because my phone is private and unlisted. God does work in a wondrous way. We talked about my letter, and her book "Broken to be Blessed." She gave me all the information I needed and asked if I would like her to send me a copy of her book. I told her "Yes." I was very glad she did, I read it twice, it was blessing to me.

✠ ✠ ✠

Chapter 3

Bucky Beaver

Bucky Beaver. What a cruel name! I remember being called that in grade school. I had a bad over bite and the kids, being kids, gave me that hurtful name. To this day I do not like my picture taken. When I was called that name, I would fight and call back names. I knew it would only make things worse for me, but I was only defending my pain. There was a lot of pain, and a lot of tears. I grew older fighting back at anyone that I thought was going to hurt me or my Sissy. The older I got the fouler the words. I'm not at all proud of that, as a matter of fact I am still ashamed. Even today people remember me as being a hateful and ugly person. I wanted to get you, before you got me. I want to apologize to all the people I hurt with my cruel words. The only excuse I have was ignorance. Please forgive me; I am not the same person today. I am a child of God, and He has made me a new creation. Not perfect, I still have a temper when you talk against my Lord, my family and friends, my country, but God has shown me how to hold back when I should, and how to use my words. If I, or I should say when I slip, God will gently convict my spirit, and I repent. Besides, retaliation really never made me feel better, I always feel sick to my stomach.

My Dad took me to the dentist to have a tooth pulled; the dentist told him I needed braces to straighten my teeth. I remember feeling excited that the kids wouldn't be calling me names anymore. But it was not to be. Daddy asked how much the braces would cost. I don't know what it was but I do know Daddy said, "I cannot afford that, maybe someday but not now." I wanted to cry. Daddy took my hand and we got into the car. I asked, "Daddy, am I going to get my teeth fixed?" He looked at me and said, "No Reety, Daddy just doesn't have the money." I started to cry again, partly from the pain of the pulled tooth. He said, "Now just stop crying, I can't do it that ends it!"

But it didn't end it for me. I was fortunate to have a Christian Mother, and to belong to the Belle Center Methodist Church, where they had Sunday school teachers that taught you scriptures about a God that answered prayers.

I remember one teacher in particular. Miss Bernice Young. She taught the youth group. She told us if we learned by memory the 23rd Psalm, The Lords Prayer, (Luke 11:2) and John 3:16, we would each receive a New Testament Bible. I memorized, and stood in front of the class and repeated all the scriptures, and I proudly received my reward. I have the New Testament Bible to this day.

When I was in the 5th grade, I had a crush on a boy in my class. My best friend told him, and it wasn't long after that he was embarrassing me in front of the whole class. He told me I was ugly and he hated people with buck teeth. The boys in class all laughed at me, I was so humiliated. There it was again, that ugly name! I just wanted to run away and hide. But I didn't, I came back with "I don't like you you're a real puke!" Real cool, huh.

I remember going home after school, crying and going into Mom's bedroom and sitting in front of her dressing table, adjusting the mirrors so I had a clear view of my face, my ugly face. I looked at myself for awhile. Then asking God, "Why did you make me so ugly? Please straighten my teeth. My daddy doesn't have the money, and they call me Bucky Beaver and it hurts. Jesus, please make me pretty so I'm not laughed at anymore. And Jesus don't get mad at me, but I would like to have dimples, they don't have to be big ones, but when I smile little ones show right here. (I pointed to the spot across from the corner of my mouth.) Jesus, Id like a small dimple in my chin too. Thank you."

As a child I only knew to pray and believe God would give me what I wanted. I never told anyone I had asked Jesus to straighten my teeth. I guess I thought you prayed and kept it to yourself, so it was my secret. I did know, even at the age of eleven, I loved God and He was the only one that could help me.

I would return to that mirror many times, looking for my straightened teeth. I never stopped believing. Then one day, when I was fifteen years old, I went into Moms bedroom and I sat down in front of the mirror, adjusted the side mirrors and looked at my reflection. I didn't see teeth over my bottom lip anymore! I laughed, and what did I see? Two small dimples right where I had placed my fingers, and one in my chin! God had heard and answered my prayer, and in His time granted my request. God heard the child like faith I had, and my broken heart.

Jesus loves little children, He hears all their prayers. Sometimes right away, sometimes, as in my case, many years later. But He hears! He knows the right time. I'm so thankful I was taught at an early age God loves me, and not to be afraid to go to God in prayer. I saw mom pray, and that helped me to know it was okay to ask God for help. We need to let our children see us pray, and to teach them how to pray at an early age. Their faith will grow stronger over the years.

But we must also teach them God will not answer a prayer if it is going to do harm to them or others. God loves everyone, I know that is how God has worked in my life, and I have received so many blessings.

✠ ✠ ✠

Chapter 4

I Love You

It was Sunday morning in the Belle Center Methodist Church. We were singing the hymn "Abide With Me", when all of a sudden I had the strangest feeling come over me. I never had such a feeling before. It was as if something was telling me to look at the picture of Christ hanging behind the pulpit. I have always liked the picture, but I was never drawn to it as I was on this morning. All of a sudden I began to cry, the tears rolled down my cheeks. This had never happened before either. Then I heard a soft voice say, "I love you." It seemed to be coming from the picture. I felt odd, and I tried to look down at the hymnal, but my eyes would not leave the picture. Again I heard the voice say to me "I love you." I was still crying when I realized Reverend Elwood was looking at me. I looked around me and I was the only one still standing. I felt embarrassed as I sat down, but I continued to look at the picture of Jesus through the service.

I couldn't wait to get home so I could tell my mother what had happened. I knew she would have an explanation as to what I had experienced. I told mom I thought God wanted me to be a missionary, and I was going to become a Catholic. Mom said, "I don't think so! You don't have to become a catholic to be a missionary. What brought this on?" I told her about the voice I had heard saying "I love you." and how I couldn't control my tears, and the strange feeling I had felt. I told her I knew God was talking to me. Mom said, "God does talk to people, but that doesn't always mean He wants them to become missionaries, or to change their religion." She suggested I wait a few years and see what happened.

We had bought our house from missionaries that were being sent to Africa, when I was about nine years old; I was so fascinated by that. I often wished I could be a missionary to Africa too.

From the time I could read I would read the Bible to mom every chance I got. I would follow her around the house wherever she would go. She never asked me to stop bothering her, or made me feel like I was a nuisance. She would correct me when I made a mistake in any names or places, and she always could explain what I did not understand. Mom was my first Bible teacher. She truly loved the Word of God; she never got tired of hearing it even from a child.

Mom was raised in a Christian home with a bible believing mother. Grandma Houchin was a God fearing woman that knew how to pray. She was a member of the First Church of God in Bellefontaine, Ohio. It was in her church I first saw people raise their hands toward heaven, Praise God, and say Hallelujah, and call each other brother and sister.

I knew mom would be discussing with Grandma what had happened in church, and I wanted her too. I knew Grandma would be praying for me, she and mom were big on prayer. I often saw mom in prayer for her family. I learned at an early age to go to God in prayer for any need I had.

In Exodus 3; 2-4, God used a burning bush to get the attention of Moses. In Number 22; 28, God opened the mouth of a donkey to get the attention of Balaam. He used a picture to get my attention. God can and will use whatever means is needed to get His message to us. "Are you listening?"

My cousin Judy, whom I love like, and think of as a sister, gave me a praying hands necklace when I was a teenager. I wore it all the time. One day I realized it was gone. The chain must have broken and slipped off my neck. I don't think Judy ever knew how much that gift meant to me. I searched everywhere, but it was not to be found.

A few days later I went to the drug store, and I saw a gold cross necklace. I bought it and I have worn a cross everyday since. No, it Isn't a token to me, nor do I worship it. The cross is a reminder to me daily how much God loves me, and to what a degree He was willing to go so that I could be saved. Wearing a cross is my testimony of my love for my Lord and Saviour Jesus Christ. I wear my cross proudly, with love. When I am asked if I am religious I boldly say, "No, I'm a Christian, I serve and have a relationship with Jesus Christ." Jesus could have refused to be beaten beyond recognition, spit upon and hung on that rugged cross, and die, but He knew I couldn't be saved if He refused. He loved me too much to refuse the cross, and I love Him and will not refuse or deny Him. The cross means love to me, what does it mean to you?

Years passed and I got married. I stopped going to church every Sunday, but I never stopped reading my Bible. One day a bible salesman came to the door, he had a set of four books I really wanted. I felt like God had sent him to our house. I had been having a feeling that I needed more knowledge of the Bible than I had. When I saw the set with the encyclopedia I had to have it. I remember the price was $30.00. At that time we had a baby, but not much money. I didn't think Doug would buy it, so I didn't tell him how much I wanted that set. But God works in wondrous ways, and he put it upon Doug's heart to get it for me. I asked him later why he bought it, and he said he knew I wanted it. Not only did God show him the set to by, when the time came to pay for them we had no shortage of money. I have used the encyclopedia many times over in my studies of God's word.

I didn't know why God spoke to me on that Sunday morning, but I did know deep in my Spirit there was something He wanted me to do. Over the years I had three children, and I want all three to love, and have a close relationship with God.

I began to visit different churches, but what I was looking for just wasn't in any of them. Not to say they weren't good churches, they were, I just hadn't found what I needed to fill the empty place in my heart. The problem was I didn't know what I was looking for, a closer walk with God most certainly. But I felt like I was hungry, starving, but not for physical food. I couldn't explain it to anyone, because I didn't understand it myself, and I just got hungrier and hungrier. I continued reading and studying my bible and prayed someday I was going to find what I was searching for. I love God and I would never forget the day I first heard Him say "I love you."

> **"For God so loved the world, that He gave his only begotten son, that whosoever believeth in Him should not perish but have everlasting life"**
>
> **John 3:16**

That is love!

✠ ✠ ✠

Chapter 5

What's Behind The Curtain?

In May of 1975, I had a dream about walking into a hospital room. There was a big heavy gray curtain pulled around the bed next to the window. I didn't want to pull back the curtain, because I knew there was something ugly and terrible behind it. Yet, I knew I had to face whatever it was. Just as I was about to touch the curtain to pull it back I woke up.

A few days later I went to my parent's home. I told my mom about the dream, and how real it was. She looked at me with a look of shock and gave a sigh and then she asked, "God would tell you if anything were wrong, wouldn't He?" She knew God had spoken to me many times in my dreams and prayers. The look on her face told me there was something very wrong. When I asked if she was okay she said yes and changed the subject. I knew mom wasn't feeling well, but she always said it was because of her arthritis, and she was having a lot of pain in her hands and feet. No one in the family had any reason not to believe her.

A few days later my sister, Merlena, and our dad came to my house. I asked where mom was and Merlena said, "In the hospital." I looked at dad, but he didn't say anything, he just looked down at the ground. I had a sick fearful feeling in my stomach. I gave Merlena a look and she said, "Mom was in so much pain this morning, I took her to the doctor and he put her right in the hospital." She looked at dad then back at me and said, "She has breast cancer." I asked, "Why didn't you tell me this morning mom was in the hospital?" She said, "Mom said not to tell you since you are going in for surgery this week, she didn't want you to be upset." It was just like mom to think of me before herself. Mom had hidden the cancer from everyone including dad.

I went to the hospital as soon as I could. When I walked into her room my dream came to reality. Her bed was next to a window, and a heavy gray curtain was drawn around it. As I reached up to open the curtain my heart began to race, and I felt the fear I had in my dream. I prayed to God to help me, and give me the strength to face whatever was behind the curtain. Although I already knew the terrible thing I had to face was cancer, I was not prepared for the ugly. I pulled back the curtain, and mom said, "Come here, Baby, I need to show you something." She opened her gown and showed me her breast. She said, "I want you to see what trying to hide cancer will do to you. Never do this, promise me if you ever find a lump you will go to a doctor." I told her I would.

Mom had her surgery the next morning, and I checked in to the hospital for my surgery scheduled for the next morning.

The Doctor told us the cancer had spread through her body, and she only had three months to live. The nurses were very kind to me, and told me I could spend as much time in mom's room as I wanted. I spent most of that night by her bed just talking and reading the Bible to her, just like when I was at home. It was a good time for both of us. A gift from God. I'm thankful I was given that special time with mom.

I was twenty-seven years old, and I didn't want to lose a minute with her. I felt like a little girl again, afraid but I couldn't let anyone know. I learned a lot about faith and strength that night.

After mom went home, my sister and I took care of her day and night. It was so hard to watch her slip away. She wasn't only my mother; she was truly my best friend. I could go to her with any problem, and never be judged or made to feel like I was a stupid person. Mom loved me unconditionally.

God comforted me many times in many different ways while I was in that valley. I was told after my surgery I couldn't help care for my mom because I was not to do any lifting, or be on my feet for awhile. I told my surgeon I'd be careful, but I was going to take care of my mother. I asked God to give me the strength to do whatever had to be done to make mom as comfortable as we could. God answered my prayer. I never grew weak. I thank God for His compassion.

It is God that girdeth me with strength, and maketh my way perfect.

Psalm 18: 32

I read the Bible to mom every chance I got. It was really very comforting to both of us. Mom had been a Sunday school teacher for the young children for as long as I could remember. So I asked where her favorite books were in the Bible. She said, "Oh baby, I love all the bible, its all good." I asked her even though I knew the answer, if she loved Jesus, and she said, "Oh, my yes!" I just needed to hear her say it one more time.

The day she slipped into a coma we had prayed and repeated the 23rd Psalm, and the Lords Prayer. Afterwards she reached up to Heaven, looking out the window, smiled and spoke to someone softly; only she could see and hear. Then she turned to me and said, "I'm so tired baby, I want to go to sleep now, I love you." I said okay, gave her a kiss and told her I loved her. I held her hand as she quietly slipped into a coma. I felt such a strong sense we were not alone. It was a feeling of love. I would experience that feeling many more times to come. I sat for awhile just watching her breathing; mom had such a different look on her face now. A look of peace, and no pain. I knew God had answered another prayer for me. Earlier that morning I asked God to take her suffering away and just let her slip into a coma where there would be no more pain.

He shall enter into peace: they shall rest in their beds

Isaiah 57: 2

Dad asked me to ride in the ambulance with mom to the hospital. I felt the same comforting presence with us, as I had before. I thank God for answering my prayer, I kissed mom on her forehead and told her soon she was going to be with Jesus. I told her in between my tears, I loved her, and I'd see her again in heaven. I looked up at the EMT and she had tears in her eyes, she quickly looked away. I sit on the floor and held moms hand. I'd miss never hearing her call me "Baby" again.

My brothers Jim and Chuck were called, and my aunt Laura came to tell her little sister good bye. After she left I pulled my chair up beside mom's bed. I began to pray and asked God to tell me exactly when mom would die, to prepare me and to show me she went to heaven.

Ask me of things to come.

Isaiah 45: 11

I didn't know how God would answer this prayer, I just knew He would. God spoke to me so plainly, "your mother's spirit will leave her body at 1:30 a.m.

Then shall the dust return to the earth as it was;
and the spirit shall return unto God who gave it.

Ecclesiastes 12: 7

I didn't say anything to my family because I felt it was not the right time. With the exception of my mom, no one really believed God spoke to me. They all knew how much I loved the Lord and how strong my faith was. At 1:00 a.m. I told dad God said mom would die at 1:30. The boy's were sitting on the bed behind me, and Sis was standing at the foot of mom's bed with dad. He told me to stop it, so I didn't say anything more. Thinking back on it, God did not tell me to share with my family what He had told me.

I continued to pray to the Lord for strength and help for my family. Mom was always the center of love in our family, and for anyone that knew her. I looked at my watch; it was 1:25 a.m. All of a sudden I was picked up out of the chair I was sitting on, and put onto my knees. I went into tongues very briefly. I suddenly stopped and looked at mom. I felt the strong presence of God. There was the brightest white light I had ever seen streaming through the window across my dads shoulder. Not touching him but, onto moms chest. I said, "Do you see it? Do you see it?" Dad said, "What?" I said, "The light!" he said, "No." I said, "Praise God, thank you Jesus, thank you." The light was gone and mom was no longer breathing. It all happened so fast. I said, "God was here and took mom to heaven." Everyone just stood there, not saying a word, so I went to get a nurse to tell her mom was gone.

Later my brother, Chuck, told me, "Boy, you sure came out of that chair fast and on your knees." I asked, "You saw that?" Chuck said, "Yes it looked like someone was behind you and picked you up and sat you on your knees. I've never seen anything like it before." I asked if he saw the bright light that was shining on mom. He said, "No, I wish I had." I wish they all could have.

I'm thankful God granted me the favor of seeing His holy light. I know God opens the eyes of those who believe, and want to see. I thank Him for opening my eyes.

The hearing ear, and the Seeing Eye, the Lord hath made even both of them.

Proverbs 20: 12

The Lord took my mother home at 1:30 a.m., June 9, 1976.

✠ ✠ ✠

Chapter 6

Jesus I Don't Want To Go Back

In 1978, I had a stomach biopsy done; when I came around I was back in my room. I remembered being with Jesus. We were standing on an arc shaped, pure white stone bridge talking. Jesus was wearing a pure white brilliant robe with a golden sash around His waist. Hanging down from the sash was what looked to me like a long golden chain or cord. At the end was something attached to it but I couldn't make it out, due to the fold of His robe. He had the sweetest voice I've ever heard. Jesus was pointing out to me things around us, things that bring me joy here on Earth.

There was a green pasture, the shade of which I have never seen here on Earth. The flowers were of every color and bright. The smell was a sweet and calming scent. A perfect tree, large beyond description, the limbs were filled with so many lush green leaves. It made the tree look like a huge bouquet. The brook of running water below us was crystal clear. I could see white rocks lying at the bottom; there was no mud on the bottom. It looked to me like they were lying on diamond dust. Everything was clear and clean. The light was brilliant, but it didn't hurt my eyes. Everything I saw had a feel of love.

As Jesus and I talked He was telling me I had to go back for now, but someday this would all be mine. My house was not yet built. As He took His hand and slowly pointed it all out to me again. I told Jesus I didn't want to go back. I kept repeating, "Jesus, Jesus, I don't want to go back."

The surgical nurse came into my room, still wearing her surgical greens. She asked "how I was feeling," and then she took my pulse. I was wondering what the surgical nurse was taking my pulse for. I told her "I was okay". She asked "if I felt like talking?" I told her, "yes". She looked me in the eye and said, "I'm here to apologize to you." I asked, "for what?" She said, "For slapping you so hard on the face." She then touched my cheek and asked, "I didn't hurt you did I? I don't see any bruising." I laughed and told her "no". She then asked, "You're a Christian aren't you?" I said "yes". She said, "I thought so, I am to. While you were on the table we almost lost you, your blood pressure dropped so low we had to stop the surgery until it came back up. Then while you were in the recovery room I couldn't get you to wake up. You just kept saying 'Jesus, I don't want to go back.' I knew if I didn't get you awake we would lose you, so I had to repeatedly slap you in the face. I was calling your name, but you just kept saying Jesus' name over and over until I slapped you really hard. I'm very sorry, but I knew you were talking to Jesus, and you didn't want to leave Him."

She asked me if I would tell her what it was like to be with Jesus. I told her about all I had seen, and that Jesus had pointed things out to me, how we talked, His sweet voice, and the loving feeling that surrounds everything, and how He told me I had to go back for now, but I really wanted to stay with Jesus. She thanked me for sharing my visit to heaven with her. She left my room and I never saw her again. A few months later I heard one of the surgical nurses had died of cancer.

> In my Father's house are many mansions; if it were not so, I would have told you. I go to prepare a place for you.

> And if I go and prepare a place for you, I will come again, and receive you unto myself: that where I am there ye may be also.
>
> John 14: 2, 3
>
> (KJV)

✠ ✠ ✠

Chapter 7

I'll never forget

I had a dream I was planting flowers in a flower bed at the house I was raised in. The sidewalk was broken and a big piece of concrete was sticking up. My brother came walking up to me, and I said, "Be careful, Chucky, don't trip over that broken sidewalk." He looked at me, and smiled, before he tripped and fell. He hit his head really hard. I went to him and blood was streaming down his face. I cradled his head in my lap, and began wiping his face. I said, "Oh Chucky, oh Chucky, open your eyes, I love you!" I woke up asking God what it meant.

The night of April 14, 1984 became a night of shock and unanswered questions, and to me of great loss. That was the night I received a phone call from sister telling me our brother, Chuck, was dead.

I don't want to go into a lot of detail about my brother's death, because I wasn't there and anything I might say would be second hand. What I do know is someone I loved is gone forever and I miss him.

Anyone that knew Chuck knew he had his own personal demons, but no matter how hard he tried to be free of them he couldn't. He had a good heart. He gave to anyone in need and neither asked or wanted anything in return.

A few days before Chuck died we were at our dad's house, and he began to rub his forehead. I asked "if his head was bothering him?" He said "he had been having awful headaches again and some leakage from an old surgical incision between his eyes." Years earlier he had a tumor attached to the front of his brain. The tentacles were growing down into his forehead and the bridge of his nose. I remember how awful the pain was and there was no medication that could touch it. I didn't want him going through that hell again. They put a plate in his forehead and nose and he was told to be careful not to take a hit to that area. I asked if he had been to the doctor. He just said there was nothing to be done for the pain. I asked him what he meant. He said, "I'll be alright, Sis, don't worry about me."

We talked about a lot of things that day. About his job, how much he really liked what he was doing and that he was good at it, how much he loved his three kids, and how he loved taking his son fishing at the old creek. Chuck loved hunting and fishing. He even did some trapping. He told me about a special place he went to in the woods that opened into a field. He liked to go there and sit under the trees and talk to God. He said with the sun shining through the branches it was like being in his own private church. He said he would tell people he was going fishing, but he really was spending time with God, and he wanted to be alone. I was so touched; Chuck felt he could share a personal moment as that with me.

He got up from the kitchen table, gave me a long tight hug and a kiss on the top of my head. When he lifted his head there were tears falling down his cheeks. I said, "Chucky, I love you and I have never been ashamed to call you my brother." He said, "I know Sis." He squeezed my shoulder, walked to the door, stopped looked at dad, and back at me. Waved good bye and winked at me. That was his signature way of saying good bye. I had such a heavy sadness come over me, a feeling I was never going to see him again. I jumped up from the chair and ran to the door. I called out to him as he was getting into his car. "Chucky, I love you!" We looked at each other for a few seconds. I remember thinking I wish I had a camera. Then he waved good bye, winked again and he drove away. I asked dad, "He won't do anything will he?" Dad shook his head no.

I answered the phone and the first words I heard were, "Marieta, Chuck shot himself tonight." I thought my heart would stop beating, my chest hurt so badly. It felt like the wind had been knocked out of me. I whispered, "God, oh God!" I took a breath and asked, "Is he okay?", and my sister said "no". I asked "if he was dead", fearing the answer. She said, "yes". Between the tears I asked "if he suffered?" She said, "No he died almost instantly." She then said, "Chuck said, Oh, my God." before he died.

I called out to God over and over. My legs grew weak and I fell to the floor. My husband, Doug, heard me and came into the dining room, took a look at me and asked what was going on. I told him "Chuck was dead." I couldn't stand. He helped me to a chair, took the phone and spoke to Sissy for a few minutes and hung up. He said, "Merlena is coming over, she wants to be with you tonight." I was beginning to feel numb, I felt a deep sadness come over me. A great loss, it was almost unbearable. I whispered, "Jesus, help me." I prayed until she got here, putting myself in God's hands. What else could I do? God was the only one that could give me the comfort I needed now.

There have been many times like now writing this down and remember the heart break of losing Chuck. I have to call on the Lord for comfort, for myself and all who loved him. Jesus is only a prayer away. He never refuses to answer the call. What a loving and compassionate Lord we serve.

> **Fear thou not; for I am with thee; be ye not dismayed; for I am thy God; I will strengthen thee; yes, I will help thee; yea, I will uphold thee with my right hand of my rightousness.**
>
> **Isaiah 41:10**

I often think about Chuck and his last words. I pray he was calling out to God. I can only hope he is where there is no pain, or tears, no memories of things lost and no sadness. Only joy. I thank God; heaven is a place where we never know if our loved ones didn't make it there. God alone knows for sure if I will see my brother again. I love you Chucky and I will never forget you.

> **And God shall wipe away all tears from their eyes; and there shall be no more death, neither sorrow, nor crying, neither shall there be any more pain; for the former things are passed away.**
>
> **Revelation 21: 4**

I am so thankful to God that He allowed me to tell Chuck one last time I love him, and Chuck was able to tell me one last time he loved me. I have been comforted many times by the memory of those words. I try to never leave someone I care about without telling them, 'I love you!'

✠ ✠ ✠

Chapter 8

I Love You More

When I first found out I was going to have our third child, the Lord told me I was going to have a boy. I was told by a family member, "You don't know that for sure, girls run in the family not boys, you have two girls and you will have a third." It didn't make any difference how many people tried to tell me I didn't hear from God, I knew what I heard and I knew who I heard it from.

After months of problems with my pregnancy and having my labor induced, and a difficult delivery, on September 20, 1971, weighing in at 8 lbs. Eric Douglas Collins was born.

From a month old he began having convulsions, accompanied with spiking fevers of 102. When Eric was a little over a year old, he woke me up in the middle of the night, burning up with fever and having the worst convulsion yet. We rushed him to the hospital. They began packing him in ice to bring down the fever of 106. I was sitting outside the cubicle, behind a curtain. I could hear everything they were doing and saying. I kept praying for God to help my baby. All of a sudden I heard one of the nurses say, "We are losing him! I can't find his heartbeat anymore." The other nurse said, "Shh, his mother can hear you!" Then I heard the first nurse say, "We lost him, he is gone." In tears I told God, "I love my baby, and I don't want him to die. But I love you more. You gave him to me, now I'm giving him back to you." As soon as I spoke those words, I heard the nurse say, "He's back, I've got a heartbeat again!" I began thanking Jesus for saving my baby boy.

I was told Eric might have some brain damage, due to the high fever and his heart stopping. I refused to accept that lie. God was in control of my son's health, not Satan. Since my conception, Satan has tried to bring harm to my son. God has intervened in each attempt, from illness, being hit in the face by a fastball in high school, knocking him out and giving him a concussion, to almost being swept away by flood waters, to car wrecks. Only God and Eric know what else.

God always tells me when to pray for Eric, in dreams, by speaking to me, or by a leading of the Holy Spirit speaking to my spirit, with a certain feeling I have become to know. God does this with all my children and grandchildren.

I have always believed God has a plan for Eric's life.

As for the possible brain damage he was supposed to have. Eric was in Who's Who among American High School Students. He was very good in sports, received the Most Valuable Player award in football his senior year. Graduated Salutatorian of his class in 1990. Graduated from Ohio State University, School of Business in 1995. He has done very well in the business world. What Satan meant for harm and my heart break, God has made into many Testimonies to His glory and great love! What a great God! I'll serve him forever! I love our Lord!

✠ ✠ ✠

Chapter 9

Pray for those Boys!

On March 24, 1988, my husband and I bought our son, Eric, a 1969 Nova. I took one look at this car and I had a bad feeling about it. I told Doug and Eric I didn't like this car, and I wished he had a different one. Eric said, "Oh mom you worry too much." I prayed asking God to protect Eric when he was in that car, that no harm comes to him or anyone riding in it. Eric didn't have his driver's license yet so the Nova sat in the driveway like a big bad sign. I prayed a lot over that car.

On May 31st, my sixteen year old son got his drivers license. He was so happy he could now drive to school. No more bus and mom didn't have to drive him to ball practice anymore. Eric also started his first job at McDonalds on June 1st.

Everything went fine until the afternoon of June 7th. One of Eric's friends came out to our house. Eric asked if it was okay if they took a ride. They wanted to go to a friends, just a couple miles away. I told them yes, but to be careful. As soon as they backed out of our driveway I had a familiar feeling, and fear came over me. I looked out the picture window and yelled, "Eric, stop! Don't go!" I knew he couldn't hear me but it was just a reaction. I said, "Oh, God!" I heard a familiar soft voice; it was the Holy Spirit speaking to me. He said, "Pray! Pray for those boys now!" I didn't hesitate; I knew I had heard from God.

**Cease not to cry unto the Lord our God for us,
that He will save us out of the hand of the Philistines.
1 Samuel 7: 8**

I began praying for protection around the boys, that the devil get his hands off the car, and the boys. I prayed and prayed until a peace came over me. Just moments later the phone rang. I glanced at the clock. I had been in prayer for an hour. I answered the phone, it was Eric. He said, "Mom, I'm on 190, I wrecked the car and I need you to come." I asked if he was hurt and if his friend was okay. He said no one was hurt but he needed me to bring his proof of insurance, he had totaled his car. I began thanking God and praising His name for saving those boys.

When I got to the sight of the accident I began thanking God all over again. Both boys were out walking around the car looking at it. Totaled was a good word for what I saw.

Eric was driving too fast, lost control on the curve, and went between a guide wire on an electric pole, hit a farmer's fence post, and ended up in his hay field.

The State Patrolman asked, "Do you realize how lucky these boys are?" I said, "Yes." He said, "Ma'am, I don't think you do." He walked me through the skid marks on the curve of the road, straight between the guide wire and pole. He said, "Ma'am, you could have lost your son, I don't know why you didn't. If they had hit that guide wire instead of going between it and the pole, which I don't understand why they didn't, that car could have been cut in half and those boys killed. All I can say is someone was watching over those boys." I told him "God was watching over them."

Eric only had a few cuts and bruises, his friend didn't have any cuts but I'm sure he had bruises. As for the car, the front axle was broken, the left front fender and door were smashed in. The fan went through the radiator; the transmission was pushed up into the car. Totaled? Yes. A miracle? Most definitely.

I thank God for telling me to pray for those boys, and I obeyed the command. God is good and merciful.

> **But the mercy of the Lord is from everlasting upon them that fear Him, and His righteousness unto children's children.**
>
> **Psalm 103: 17**

> **For He shall give His angels charge over thee, to keep thee in all thy ways**
>
> **Psalm 91: 11**

✠ ✠ ✠

Chapter 10

Did I Do The Right Thing?

My dad had hernia surgery, but for some reason he was having a lot of pain in his left leg. He went back into the hospital for more tests.

The morning of March 21st, 1991, I received a call from the hospital. The nurse said, "Your dad isn't doing very well, can you call the family and come as soon as you can?" I asked what was wrong, but she wouldn't tell me. I called and left a message for my brother, Jim, at his work place, telling him to go to the hospital as soon as he could. There was something wrong with dad. Them I called my sister Merlena.

When we got to the hospital they wouldn't let us in dad's room. The crash cart was sitting in front of the door, and we could see the doctor and nurses were in his room working on him. Jim arrived before sissy and I got there, and was sitting in the hall. I asked him what had happened. Jim said, the nurse told him she was getting dad ready to go down for the last round of x-rays before discharging him. Then all of a sudden he grabbed his chest and said he couldn't stand the pain. Then he just collapsed. I asked Jim what were they doing and what was the crash cart doing there, and they wouldn't let us see him. He said he didn't know, he was told that the doctor would be out to talk to us.

After what seemed like an eternity the Doctor came out into the hall. He said, "For some reason you dads left lung collapsed, pushing air through his chest, and causing his heart to stop beating. The staff and I worked on your dad for twenty minutes getting his heart started again. We reinflated his left lung and stabilized him, and put him on a ventilator. They are taking him to intensive care."

Dad had congestive heart failure and arterial disease. He had one heart attack years earlier and they had to restart his heart. He said he would never go through that again. He also had lost his right lung to emphysema. Dad had a living will made out several months earlier, making me power of attorney concerning anything medical. Jim was power of attorney concerning anything financial. Dad made me promise, if anything like this happened I wouldn't let them put him on any kind of life support or to resuscitate him. But I wasn't at the hospital when he collapsed, and they did not pay any attention to what was in his file.

When I found out he was on a ventilator I asked why, when dad had a living will in his file. I was told there wasn't one. I told the nurse I knew better. I had given it to the nurse the day dad was admitted. I looked at the nurse and took out the copy I had in my purse. I handed it to the Doctor and said, "Take him off the machine." The doctor said, "No, I did what I felt was right." I said, "But you knew dad had a living will." The Doctor said he was sorry, but that it was hospital policy if there were no family members present, it was the Doctors decision. I had known this doctor for twenty years, I knew he had a kind heart and would do all he could for dad. But this was not what he wanted, and I made him a promise I would not let this happen, and my word means something to me.

Dad was in seizures for twelve hours before they found the right medication to stop them. I asked if he was in any pain since he was in a coma. We were told they really did not know. Jim told them to find something to help with the seizures, because dad had a very bad back and neck, and he would be in unbearable pain. We couldn't stand to see him having these seizures. We all three felt so helpless and like we were in a very bad dream.

I continued trying to get dad off the machine. I asked every day, but the answer was the same. We were told the ventilator was keeping dads lung from collapsing again. The machine was keeping dad alive. That was not dads wishes, this was tearing me up inside.

Dad's doctor was very kind to me, even though I had told him he was not God. He knew how I felt about his decision. Every day after he visited dad he would sit and talk with me. One day he told me how sorry he was for putting dad on a ventilator, but he had just gone through the same thing with his dad, and thought it was the right thing to do. He told me he would run an EEG to see if dad had any active brain waves, and then take it from there.

In those eight days and nights I walked the hall, and I prayed, I sat by dads bed holding his hand praying and telling him how very sorry I was for failing him, and I was doing everything I could to help him.

I prayed to Jesus for guidance and strength. I needed so much to hear from Him. I knew He was with me, because I could feel His sweet presence. I was standing on God's holy word He would never forsake me. He hadn't yet, and I knew He was right beside me now. I knew Jesus would speak to me in His own time.

I knew I had to keep fighting this battle. I loved my dad and I didn't want him to continue going through what he was now. I made a promise, and I was going to keep it, with my Lords help.

We knew the machine was breathing for him, and his body had already sustained more than it had too. Everyday they were telling us they wanted to do something else. I wanted them to put dad in Gods hands.

The morning of the ninth day, I felt so weary, and I was alone so I sat down in a chair outside of the ICU. I broke down and cried. I asked God to please help me. I was only doing what dad had asked me to do for him. I felt so sad, what an awful thing to have to fight for, and what a heavy burden I had been given. But I knew God would never give me more than I could bear. I knew He was watching me and if I began to stumble He was there to catch me.

As I was sitting there praying, a lady asked if I was Leo Miller's daughter. I told her I was. She then told me she was from the administrations office and asked where my brother and sister were. I told her they were at work but would be back later. She said she saw where Marieta Collins was Leo's power of attorney. "Is that you?" she asked. I told her, "Yes, is something wrong?" She told me they needed dad's bed to be freed up, and since he wasn't getting any better they wanted to give him a trache and put him in a special room in the basement until we could get him in a nursing home. She said she didn't mean to be cruel but he wasn't going to be able to stay in ICU indefinitely. I told her, no they were not going to trache him and I reminded her, the hospital made the mistake by putting dad on the ventilator to begin with. She said, "Well talk it over with your family and let me know your decision."

I couldn't take it anymore, I needed Gods help. I asked God if I was wrong to keep fighting this battle to please show me, and if I wasn't wrong and this was not his will for dad to be kept alive this way to please show me.

A nurse came out and saw me sitting there. She sat down beside me. I told her I loved my dad and didn't want him to die, but I knew his wishes. Then I asked her point blank, how can a 78 year old man live without his lungs, and a heart so bad it doesn't want to keep beating on its own? She patted my hand and said, "He can't." Then she got up and said, "I'll talk to the doctor for you."

I went in to see Dad and pray for him again, and then I went back out and sat down. About and half an hour later the Doctors and the same nurse came to me and said, "We will turn off the ventilator, but only if you understand what this means." I assured them I did. They said, "We have done all we can for your dad, but we want to do one more EEG to check his brain waves one more time to see how much he has declined. Then we will turn off the ventilator." I told them okay.

By that afternoon the EEG had been done. Merlena had come from work and together we waited for what was to come next. Neither of us had much to say to each other. I think our mourning had begun; at least it had for me. Dads nurse came out with the papers; she sat down beside me and began to explain to me about the EEG results. Dad only had brain stem waves, and they were very weak. She looked at Merlena and back at me and said "he is clinically brain dead." She took my hand and said, "It is time." I looked at my sister for a moment; the nurse asked her if she wanted to sign the papers too. She shook her head no. I signed the papers. The nurse asked me if I was alright. I told her I was but I felt so sad. She said she understood, and then she told us the Doctors would be in at 6:00 to shut off the machine. I asked her if we could be with dad when they do it. She said yes if we wanted too, but they didn't know how long he would live. But we could stay with him, no one would bother us, but if we needed them they would be there for us. I thanked her for being so kind to us, and I said we really appreciated all the nurses had done in the past nine days. "God had shown me his will."

I called Jim when I knew he was off work and told him what was going on and he came as soon as he could. I began praying for strength for all of us. I knew the next few hours were not going to be easy. We all had our private time with dad, to say our goodbyes. I went back in at 8:00 p.m. and talked to dad, and prayed again. I knelt down at the foot of his bed, holding his hand, I again asked Jesus to please show me I had done the right thing in fighting to get dad off the ventilator.

As I knelt there I felt a hand touch my shoulder and a mans voice softly say, "You did the right thing." I tried to lift my head to see who had spoken to me, but it felt as if someone had put there hand on my head, and I couldn't raise it up. This only lasted a few seconds. I looked around the ICU to see who had been behind me, but the only people I saw were two nurses at the desk. They looked at me as I got up from my knees. I went to the desk and I asked "Where is the man that was talking to me?" They looked at each other, then one nurse said, "No one was here but us, would you like us to call the Chaplain? He left an hour ago but we can call him back if you need him." I said, "No thank you." Then the nurse said, "This has happened before, people saying someone has spoken to them." I told them thanks and left the ICU. I went out to the waiting room where Jim and Sissy were sitting. Jim looked at me and asked if I was okay. I shook my head yes. He said I had been in there for hours. I said, "Have I? Didn't seem like it." Then I asked if they had seen a man come out. They both said no, there hadn't been anyone there but them all night. I said I would be right back. I ran down to the elevator and went down to the snack room. I knew I wouldn't find the man because I knew I had been visited by an angel, sent from God. But my emotions were running so high I wasn't in control. I can't explain how I was feeling; I just wanted so much to see my messenger from God, who came to tell me, "You did the right thing."

Are not the angels all ministering Spirits, sent out
in the service of those who are to inherit salvation?
Hebrew 1: 14

Dad stopped breathing at 11:55 p.m. on Good Friday, March 30, 1991.

✠ ✠ ✠

Chapter 11

God, Please Send Someone

The morning of April 24ᵗʰ, 1992, I prayed and wept before the Lord, asking, no begging, Him to please send someone to me soon showing me the church He wanted me to go to. I was so hungry for Gods word. I asked for a bible preaching, Holy Spirit filled church. I felt the Holy Spirit with me that morning, and I knew in my spirit God had heard my plea.

Eighteen years earlier, two of Doug's friends, John Gill and Darrell Jolliff introduced us to the Pentecostal Church. In February 1974, with one on each side of me I received the baptism in the Holy Spirit, with the evidence of speaking in tongues.

And they were filled with Holy Spirit, and began to speak with other tongues, as the Spirit gave them utterance.

Acts 2: 4

Although I was not able to continue going to the church I never forgot how I felt when I attended. I didn't want to go home when the services were over. It was so much different than any church I had ever gone to. I learned Gods' love is Spiritual and is always here for me when I need Him. I learned I can talk to Him and He hears me. I was taught not to be afraid of God, it was alright for me to tell Him I love Him, and I can go to His throne room boldly and tell Him what I wanted and needed, and to expect to receive. I learned I am His child and He only wants what is best for me. It really sounded like what my mom had told me as a child. That was the year all my miracles began to start happening for me and my family.

I needed to be back in a church that believed, and taught that miracles did not die with the Apostles. Where the Holy Spirit was present and Jesus Christ was taught, where you heard about the cross and the blood of our Lord. Where my faith would be built up. Where I would be fed the word of God and have a closer walk with Him. I would not settle for anything less. I considered myself to be Pentecostal, and that was never going to change.

That evening while I was clearing the supper dishes, my daughter, Tonya, asked, "Mom, who is talking to Dad?" I looked out the window and told her that I didn't know who he was, After a few minutes they came into the house. My husband introduced me to Doug Copp. They had gone to school together, and now Doug was a missionary to South Africa. He and his wife Phyllis, were home visiting his family in Ridgeway. He said he had been to town and saw Doug outside and he had been led of the Lord to stop and to talk to him. I told him about my morning prayer, and how I had asked God to send someone to me. I laughed and said, "I didn't think He would send me someone from Africa though."

Doug told me about a church in Kenton called the House of Prayer. He gave me the address and told me he would call a couple of his friends that went there, and have them meet me the next Sunday. He said they were very kind people and would take me under their wing until I got to know people. He said there names were Paul and Shirley Ramsey.

After Doug left I thanked God for answering my prayer. Sunday morning I prayed before leaving for church asking God to give me a sign if The House of Prayer was where I was supposed to go. I was given a vision of a large wooden cross hanging above the altar. I asked that there be someone there I knew.

My daughter Tonya went with me, and as soon as we walked into the church sanctuary we were met by Paul and Shirley Ramsey. Just as I had been told they took us under their wing. They are truly two of the nicest people I have ever met, they are truly Christian. To this day we are not only Brother and Sister in the Lord, we are friends. I love them.

The first thing I saw as we were being seated was a large wooden cross, just as I had seen in my vision from God earlier that morning. There were also two other people I knew there. What a great God we serve.

Delight thyself also in the Lord, and He shall give thee the desires of thine heart.

Psalms 37: 4

I loved the Pastor and his wife, Jim and Betty Hollon. They were very special to me. They were always so kind and caring and taught me so much about walking with the Lord. I thank them. When you ask God to send someone to you expect someone to come. From near or far. When you ask for anything, ask believing, and you will receive.

> **And all things, whatsoever ye shall ask in prayer, believing, ye shall receive.**
>
> **Matthew 21: 22**

✠ ✠ ✠

Chapter 12

Lord, I Can't Go In There Alone

On October 27, 1992, I called my brother Jim to tell him I was grandma for the second time. My oldest daughter Tonya had given birth to a precious baby girl, Caitlin Renea, the day before. He said he was happy for me and asked how Tonya and the baby were doing. Then we began to talk about what was going on in his life. I told Jim I felt deeply that God had something planned for him. I didn't know what it was, I just felt it. Now that he was living for God maybe He was going to use him. We had such a nice talk, I was really glad I called him. I almost didn't, I was just going to send him a note, but I felt I needed to talk to him.

Jim said he had to go because he had bible classes at the Urbana College. I said, "Okay, I love you Jimmy." He said, "I love you too sis, take care."

Five days later sissy called to tell me Jim had died in his sleep the night before. I was unable to stand. My knees buckled on me, as with the news of Chuck, I went to the floor. I just couldn't have lost someone else I loved. I called out to God again; I needed Him so much at that moment. Sissy told me, J.D., Jims son had tried to call me, but he got the answering machine. He didn't want me to hear about Him in that way. She told him I was helping Tonya, and she would call me there. We cried and made our plans for getting together.

When we were finished talking, Tonya asked what was wrong. I told her Uncle Jim had died. I began crying again and she asked if I wanted her to call Betty Hollon and get the prayer chain going. I told her, "Yes, I need strength." I began asking the Lord to help me. I said, "Oh Lord Jesus, I don't have any big brothers now. They are both gone." I heard Jesus speak so tenderly, "I will be your brother when you need one."

For whosoever shall do the will of my Father which is in heaven, the same is my brother, and sister, and mother.

Matthew 12: 50

The feeling of love that came over me was so comforting. If you have never felt Gods touch of love, you are missing so very much.

I went to the funeral home alone for the family viewing. My husband was at work and I was supposed to meet sissy there. I sat in my car just staring at the door, I recalled a dream I had a few years earlier. Dad and Jim were in an accident together where they drove off a rocky cliff, and were killed. I was not able to move, I tried but I couldn't. This just didn't seem real to me. We lost Mom, Chuck, Dad and now Jim. Sissy and I are the only two left of our family. I said, "God, this is too hard. I just can't go in by myself. I'm all alone and I can't move my legs." Then I heard, "My child you are never alone. I am always with you. That's not Jim anymore. He is with me now." I began praising God and thanking Him for His help and comfort. The paralyzing feeling that had come over me was now gone. In place of it was peace. I got out of my car and I went in and told my big brother good bye for now. I know I will see Jim in heaven someday, when my time comes for God to call me home.

There have been so many times in my life that if Jesus hadn't been beside me, I know I wouldn't have been able to stand the pain and shock of the trial. I thank my Lord for His love, compassion, strength, understanding, comfort and mercy. He has never failed me and I know without a doubt He never will.

> **In my distress I cried unto the Lord and he heard me.**
>
> **Psalm 12: 1**

Jim was only 53 years old. We never know when we go to bed at night, if we will wake up in the morning on earth or in eternity. God doesn't promise us a tomorrow. That is why we need to live for Jesus each day.

> **Boast not thyself of tomorrow; for thou knowest not what a day may bring forth.**
>
> **Proverbs 27: 1**

> **Whereas ye know not what shall be on the morrow. For what is your life? It is even a vapor, that appeareth for a little time, and then vanisheth away.**
>
> **James 4: 14**

✠ ✠ ✠

Chapter 13

A Walk Through A Long Valley

In April 1993, my walk began when I found a lump in my left breast. On May 19th I went for a mammogram. Since Mom died, I had one done yearly.

After the technician took the film she left the room. When she came back she said, "I didn't find anything, but I just don't feel right about it for some reason, and I want to take another film. I'd rather be safe than to find out later I had missed something." I told her I had found a lump. She asked where it was. I showed her and she checked for herself and said, "Yes, I feel it too." She took another film, but it still was not showing up. She told me to call my doctor tomorrow. The reason the lump was not showing on the film was because it was on the outside area of where the mammogram took the film.

May 20th, I called the doctor. His nurse told me the film came back clean. I told her about the lump I had found and that the technician had felt it too. She spoke to the doctor and he said he didn't want to see me, to get right to my surgeon. The nurse called my surgeons office while I was put on hold. He was on vacation and wouldn't be able to see me until June 3rd. Doug kept saying everything was going to be alright and I didn't have cancer. I didn't argue with him, but my walk with God is close enough that I know when He is preparing me for a storm in my life. The prayers, the dreams and the talks we had been having told me, I did have cancer. But I was calm, and I really felt no fear. I knew this comfort was coming from the Holy Spirit.

June 3rd came and the surgeon scheduled surgery for a lumpectomy on the 7th. He said with my family history, he did not want to put the surgery off.

Instead of one lump, there were two. The doctor sent the biopsy to the lab, and it would be the 15th before we would know anything, but he told me he was 99% sure there was no cancer. On the 15th I went to his office for the results. He came in the exam room with the saddest look on his face. He put down my file, and said, "I'm sorry Marieta; the biopsy showed both lumps were cancerous. But I think I got it all and it was contained to the one area. The good news is we got it in the early stages. But you do have some decisions to make." I said, "Okay." Then he said, "I'm so sorry, so sorry I missed it." I looked him in the eye and told him it was alright, and I would be okay. He patted my knee and said, "I believe you, you are a strong lady." He gave me my options and told me to go home and talk them over with my husband. He set up an appointment with an oncologist for the 22nd.

When I got into my car, I started praising the Lord. I said, "Okay God, I've got cancer, good, now I can go home to heaven." I praised God all the way home. I was in tongues all the way, I felt so happy. I know that sounds crazy, or as if I am telling a lie, but it is the truth. Ever since I had my heavenly visit in 1978, I have longed to go home to be with Jesus.

I put myself in God's hands, and I told Him whatever He chose for me was okay. Either take me home or heal me. But I would rather go home. I asked God to please help my family, because this was going to be hard on them. I remember how I felt when I was told Mom had cancer.

When I got home I called the prayer chain from church. That night when Doug got home from work we talked over my options. Doug said to do what I wanted it was my body.

I called my daughters, Tonya and Christy, and asked them to come out because I had something to tell them. When they got here I told them I had breast cancer, and there Dad and I had talked it over and he told me it my was body, to do what I wanted. Tonya then asked me what I was going to do. I looked at Tonya and Christy and said, "I'm not going to do anything." Both girls looked shocked. Tonya said, fighting back tears, "Mom, you have to do something. I never got to know Grandma Miller. And I want Caitlin to get to know her Grandma. Please, do something Mom." My girl's tears were heartbreaking to me. I remembered how I felt seventeen years earlier. I promised my girls I would fight, using my faith.

On the 22nd I saw the Oncologist; he gave me the same options as my surgeon. Have a mastectomy or wait and see what happened. Chemotherapy was ruled out for me, because I am allergic to so many drugs. But he said there was another option, if I wanted to take it. I asked what it was. He said, "trying and experimental drug, he said he didn't know what it would do. It would either speed up the cancer, or I'd have other complications. I laughed and said, "No, thank you, I'll just wait and see what happens." He said he wanted me to have another mammogram in September.

September 1st, I found another lump in my breast. I put myself in Gods hand once again. I went back to my surgeon on the 7th.

He drained fluid from the lump, and told me this was going to be a long drawn out affair fighting this cancer. He set up another mammogram for December.

I was having my daily talks with Jesus, and He was always preparing me for the next step in this valley. On September 30th I had to go back to the surgeon. I had developed an infection in my left breast, under my arm and shoulder, and I had found a fourth lump. He rescheduled my mammogram for October 5th. On the 16th I went back for my results, it showed four nodules in my lymph gland. He said he wasn't sure if the cancer had spread or not. He made an appointment for November 16th for a decision to be made on what to do.

On November 2nd, while in prayer I asked the Lord to please tell me if I am going to lose my breast. Jesus told me so gently, "Not one breast but two you'll lose." I was taken back for a moment. The Doctor had never mentioned anything about the cancer being in both breasts. Then I felt the presence of the Holy Spirit, and I felt His touch. I knew he was going to be with me, and I would be alright.

On November 8th I had to move up my appointment. I was having so much pain I couldn't wait for the 16th appointment. My surgeon decided we should take off the left breast. He said he thought it would be for the best. If I had waited, in two years, I'd have full blown cancer and I probably would not survive. He still had not said anything about both breasts.

My surgery was scheduled for December 22nd. I continued reading my bible and praying to God. I knew my faith was going to be tested, but I didn't care. I knew what I knew and that was, my God would walk me through this valley. I hadn't told anyone that God had told me the cancer was spreading and I was going to

49

lose both breasts. I was in a battle and I wasn't about to allow any negativity sent my way. In Christ I had all the help I needed. I knew Satan wanted me to bow to his will and not God's and that was not going to happen.

On December 1ˢᵗ, while in prayer, I asked the Lord to please prepare me for what the surgeon may find when he operated. I can face anything as long as Jesus is beside me; telling me what His will is in the situation. God gave me these scriptures to prepare me.

> **Why is my pain perpetual, and my wound incurable which refuseth to be healed.**
> **I am with thee to save thee and to deliver thee saith the Lord.**
> **And I will deliver thee out of the hand of the wicked, and I will redeem thee out of the hand of the terrible.**
> **Jeremiah 15: 18, 20, 21**

On December 22ⁿᵈ, the morning of my surgery I got up extra early. My stomach was in knots. I needed to pray again. I had to hear God tell me I was supposed to have this surgery, that it was Gods will. Or maybe he would tell me I wasn't to have surgery at all. I really did not want it. Even though God had given me scripture and spoke to me in prayer and dreams', telling me what was going to happen. I prayed and searched the scriptures for a way out of this surgery. God gave this scripture to me.

> **God is our refuge and strength, a very present help in trouble.**
> **Psalm 46: 1**

God told me, "Yes, you are to have the surgery, I am with you!"

Doug came into the room and said it was time to go. I closed my bible, put it in my suitcase, and we left.

Just as God told me I lost both of my breasts. They called it a bilateral mastectomy, and just as God said, He was with me; He never left me to walk this long valley alone.

Although I had a bilateral mastectomy that does not in any way mean that God turned his back on me. On the contrary, Jesus was with me every step of the way. Strengthening me from beginning to the end. I thank Him and I praise His precious name. I believe for every trial God leads us through there is a reason, and He will show us that reason in His own time. I give all the glory to Him. God truly is a merciful, loving and compassionate God.

And the Lord, He it is that doth go before thee; He will be with thee, He will not fail thee. Neither forsake thee; fear not, neither be dismayed.

Deuteronomy 31: 8

✠ ✠ ✠

Chapter 14

Another Valley

On July 13, 1994, I went to my surgeon for a check up. I was told I'd have to get a yearly check up and tests run for five years after my cancer surgery, to make sure the cancer hadn't returned. I was looking forward to being able to call myself A Survivor. I was told after I had the bilateral mastectomy done, that I had an invasive form of cancer. Which means it can return again, in a different part of my body. I was told probably my lungs, brain or bones. No one knows when or where, but probably within a year. It had been thirteen months.

During this check up the surgeon found another lump. He said it was the size of a pea, but in the same area as the first two. He went on to say it could be and infection. He put me on antibiotics and told me to come back on August 30th, if the lump was still there, he would take it out.

As always, I went to Jesus, and I also asked my church to pray for me as well.

For where two or three are gathered together in my name, there am I in the midst of them.

Matthew 18: 20

I was determined to stand on my faith, God took care of me before and I knew He would again. If my faith did not waver, and I had no intention of that happening.

For we walk by faith, not by sight.

2 Corinthians 5: 7

I didn't want anymore surgery, so again I gave this trial to God. I went to the surgeon on the 30th, and he decided I needed more surgery. He scheduled it for September 12th. He said there was a 5% chance the lump is cancer and a 25% chance the cancer has spread to the breast bone and the lymph nodes under my left arm. If I had the surgery I could lose the use of my left arm.

I began asking God for guidance. I did not want anymore surgery. What I did want was a healing from God. If He wasn't going to take me home, then heal me. I'm not afraid of dying, because I know without a doubt I'm saved and going to heaven, to that beautiful place Jesus showed me. I was going to keep standing on my faith. My bible tells me Jesus Heals. I believe every word of the bible.

I am the Lord that healeth thee

Exodus 15: 26

After nine days of silence from God, I finally got my answer. I kept praying, "God if you don't give me an answer soon it is going to be too late." I forgot God is never too early or too late, He is always right on time. He has things under His control, and He does things His way, not mine.

God told me to keep holding on. I knew what I had to do. A peace came over me that I hadn't had in days. When Doug came in from doing chores that night, I told him "I've made a decision, I don't want the surgery, I'm going to call the Doctor in the morning and tell him." Doug said, "Put your faith in God."

I prayed that night asking God to lay it upon the surgeons heart, not to give me any static about my decision, and to agree with me to just have a chest x-ray done to see if the lump had grown and to see if the cancer had spread.

On September 8th I had the x-ray taken. It showed that the lump was larger, and I had nodules in the lymph gland under my left arm. I told the surgeon I wasn't having the surgery. He made me promise I would come back in October. I told him I would. I figured that I would give God time to do whatever He was going to do to heal me. I knew my healing was on the way. I felt the presence of the Holy Spirit. I also felt a peace after my decision was made. After all God told me to keep holding on.

I did have people try to talk me out of standing on my faith, but I didn't listen to them. I knew what I knew, and that was, that God would reward me for my faith, by healing me.

This was my walk. I do not suggest to anyone to go against a Doctors advice. Or not to even not go to a Doctor when you have a health problem. Always seek medical advice. How else will you know what to pray about? We need that information to be able to know how to stand against the devil. Where to direct our prayers. Remember not going to a Doctor is what the enemy wants; he doesn't want us to know what to ask for in prayer. Because that is our first step in fighting our battle. Stand, always stand but do it wisely. I had my Doctor backing me in what I was doing, I'm not saying my faith is stronger than anyone else's; I am saying I knew this was from God. It was a time of testing for me. I needed to step out in my faith. How can I comfort others if I have never been in the same valley? How can I tell others God still heals if I don't believe it for myself? God was beginning my ministry He had chosen for me.

God told me to have my mastectomy in 1993. I knew He was guiding me then, and I obeyed, just as He was guiding me now. If I had not been sure I would have had the surgery.

Make sure God is talking to you without a doubt before you make any decision. The enemy can talk to you as well; remember he is an imitator of God, a false imitator. I did a lot of praying and had a lot of other people of God praying for me as well.

My cousin Judy Ruble, who I love like a sister, called and asked, "When are you going to have your surgery?" I told her I wasn't and that I was going to put my faith in God that He was going to give me a healing. Judy said she felt it was in Gods hand, and if I had the faith to do this, then to go for it. She would have her church pray for me. Bless Judy; she has always encouraged me in whatever I do.

When I went back to see the surgeon in October, I had another x-ray taken. This time there was no sign of a lump or any nodules. God had given me what I asked Him for, a healing. I praise His Holy name. I thank Him and I give God all the Glory!

> **And Jesus answering saith unto them, have faith in God. For verily I say unto you, that whosoever shall say unto this mountain, be thou removed, and be thou cast into the sea; and shall not doubt in his heart, but shall believe that those things which he saith shall come to pass; he shall have whatsoever he saith. Therefore I say unto to you, what things soever ye desire, when ye pray, believe that ye receive them and ye shall have them.**
>
> **Mark 11: 22-24**

The Doctor held up both x-rays and pointed out the lump and nodules to me. Then he pointed out where they should have been on the second film. He said, "I don't know where they went." I said, "I do, God healed me." He looked at me and said, "I guess so."

I believe God's healings come in many forms. Through prayer, medication, surgery, standing on faith and even in death our final healing. It is all in Gods choosing, and time. He alone knows what is best for each of His children. Whatever His decision continue to praise Him and give Him glory!

✠ ✠ ✠

Chapter 15

Honey, Where Is That Brown Spot?

In March of 1998, I went to have my fifth year of being free of cancer check up. While I was there the Doctor looked at a brown spot on my right cheek. I'd it for fifteen years, and I noticed it was getting some what larger over the past few months. But I really didn't think much of it, other than how ugly it was. The Doctor called it a lesion, and said, He really didn't like the way it looked, and how large it was getting. And at the rate of speed it was growing. He said, he thought I should have it removed, and a biopsy done. But he couldn't do it because it was flesh with my skin and it would take a plastic surgeon to remove it. He set up and appointment for April. I canceled the appointment, and did what I always do. I went to my healer, Jesus Christ. I asked Jesus to remove the spot for me. On Sunday I asked my Pastor to pray for me.

My mother's birthday would have been June 2nd, so Doug and I were taking flowers to Belle Center to the cemetery to put on her grave. Doug looked at me and asked, "Honey, where did that brown spot go?" I pulled down the visor and I looked in the mirror. I began praising God and thanking Him. I told Doug I had asked God to remove the spot in April, and then I just forgot about it.

Doug said, "You have been looking in the mirror everyday and you never noticed it was gone?" I said, "You didn't either did you? I don't know when God gave me another blessing, I just know He did and I thank Him for it."

The next Sunday I gave another testimony for God's goodness. I always give God the praise and glory He is due. We all like to give gifts, but we also like to be thanked. God is no different.

Nothing is too big or too small for God to hear and answer our prayer. He loves His children. Just ask, God is always listening for our prayer to Him.

Casting all your care upon Him; for He careth for you.

1 Peter 5: 7

✠ ✠ ✠

Chapter 16

Little Blessings From God

Blessing # 1
It's a boy!
Born September 2, 1990
Seth Andrew Collins, 8 lbs. 7 oz.

Christy had break through bleeding, and false labor all through her last couple of month of her pregnancy. We almost lost our precious little boy before he was born.

I was blessed with being able to be in the delivery room coaching Christy. She did so well during her labor. But all of a sudden the Doctor told the nurse, "I have a problem, I've lost the baby's heartbeat." He looked at Christy, and told her, "When I tell you too, push as hard as you can, but not until I say too. We need to get this baby out as fast as we can." Then he looked at me and said, "Help her, Mom, now." Someway I was able to coach and pray at the same time. I was asking Jesus to please help Christy and start little Seth's heart again, and please let him be born healthy. Praise God, another prayer was answered, we got our healthy boy!

Blessing # 2
It's a girl!
Born October 16, 1992
Caitlin Renea Jordan, 7 lbs. 15 oz.

I was concerned about Tonya from the beginning of her pregnancy. Tonya has A negative blood. That meant she had to have a special kind of shot during her pregnancy to protect the baby. And after another delivery for her health. Tonya's blood pressure was too high, and she was having trouble progressing with her labor. I sat off and on by her bed and we would pray together. She lifted her hands and praised God, and thanked God for a healthy baby. We prayed the Doctor would do something. She was getting so tired. I called the Pastors wife, Betty, and asked for prayer for Tonya and my grandbaby. The Doctor finally decided to perform a C-Section. I prayed and put Tonya in the hands of Jesus. Both Mother and baby were fine. Thank you Lord for hearing and answering my prayer.

Blessing # 3
It's a Girl!
Born August 22, 1995
Rebecca Nicole Jordan, 9 lbs. 2.8 oz.

Another prebaby shot for Tonya and this time she had Gestational Diabetes, and high blood pressure. I stood on my faith that both my girls would be ok. Tonya had another C-Section. Both Mother and Baby were fine. What a blessing to hold another healthy Granddaughter in my arms, and to know my baby was safe too. God is so good! Again my prayers were answered. Thank you, Lord.

Blessing # 4
It's a Girl!
Born September 22, 1995
Shelby Christine Collins, 8 lbs. 6.2 oz.

This baby girl is truly a miracle baby. Christy was still in the labor room when things began to go wrong. Christy began heavy bleeding, and the Doctor told me, "We have a problem." Not only was Christy in trouble from the heavy bleeding, the baby's heart rate was too low and falling. The Doctor said, "I don't have time to move you in the delivery room, Christy. You should have a C-Section but there is not time to wait." I began to quietly pray in the spirit. The Doctor said he didn't want to but he was going to suction the baby out. He said it was very important the machine was shut off at the right time or the baby could die. I began to pray harder to myself asking Jesus to help the Doctor save my girls. I looked up and the Doctor was also praying as he worked. That was a comfort to see. After suctioning the baby, the nurse said "Oh, My God." The cord was wrapped twice around her little neck and she wasn't breathing, and she was purple. After getting the cord free, the Doctor handed her to the nurse and said, "Take her and make her cry." When they realized they had to deliver the baby in the labor room, all the equipment had been brought into the room, along with two extra nurses. The Doctor looked at me and said, "I'm sorry, I can't help the baby now. I have to stop Christy's bleeding, but the nurses know what they are doing."

I turned to look at my granddaughter, but all I could see were the nurses working over her little body. I turned back to the bed, and Christy looked up at me with such fear in her eyes and said, "Pray Mom!" I fought back tears, and silently went into tongues. All the while the Doctor was working to stop Christy's bleeding, he would call out to the nurses, "I want to hear that baby cry!" That was my prayer too. It took an hour to stabilize Shelby. Finally I heard the most beautiful sound. After a few more minutes the nurse smiled and asked, "Would you like to see your granddaughter, Grandma?" I said, "Oh yes I would." I will never forget how my loving Lord gave me another miracle to testify about. I thank you God!

In my distress I called upon the Lord, and cried unto my God; He heard my voice out of his temple, and my cry came before Him, even into his ears.

Psalms 18: 6

✠ ✠ ✠

Chapter 17

The Trumpet Call

I am reminded of this vision often. I truly believe God gave it to me to pass on to others as a message of Jesus soon coming. May God speak to you as He has me through this vision. To give warning, guidance, and His message of love for His children, that He would prepare us a head of time for the coming Rapture of His Church. We do not know the time or the day, but be assured Jesus return draweth nigh.

January 1993, while in prayer, God gave me this vision. I saw a beautiful angel slowly descending from heaven; it was as if he was in slow motion. In his hand he had a long golden trumpet; he was wearing a long white robe. It went down to his feet. His hair was to his shoulders, and beautiful golden color. It had a soft shine to it, and it seemed if I were to touch it the feel would be softness unknown to man. The angel looked at me for a second, and then he slowly turned his head to the side and began to slowly put the trumpet to his lips as if he were going to blow it. But then he very slowly began to fade away, without blowing the trumpet.

I quickly looked into my bible for a confirmation, and for understanding of what God had jut shown me. God quickly gave me this scripture.

And He shall send His angels with a great sound of a trumpet, and they shall gather together His elect from the four winds, from one end of heaven to the other.

Matthew 24: 31

I know in my heart God was telling me He is soon going to send His angels to gather His children. He wants us to be prepared for Christ's return. I have such a strong feeling in my spirit of the closeness of this great day. Do I think I am the only one God has given this message too? Most certainly not. I believe there are many others, the world over. Do I believe I am to share this vision at this time? Yes! The day is drawing near. Please heed the warning, get ready, and be prepared for the rapture of Gods Church.

How do you get ready? Open your heart to Jesus. Accept Him as your Savior. He is the only one that can save you from what is to come upon the earth. He went to Calvary that God would forgive your sins and be saved. Just ask Jesus to come into you heart, repent of all your sins, turn your life over to Him then look up, your redemption draweth nigh.

May God bless you!

✠ ✠ ✠

Chapter 18

Awake From Your Slumber

In April of 1995, I had a dream I was shopping, I put my items up on the check out counter. Someone behind me began talking to me. WE were laughing and talking and I wasn't paying any attention to the cashier, until she said, "Put your hand, palm up." I did as she said, while still talking and looking behind me. Just as she was going to touch my hand with a thick pencil like object, I jerked my hand away and said, "No I won't take the mark of the beast!" She said, "You have too or you can't buy these items." I said, "I don't care, I won't take the mark of the beast." I began to cry and asked God to forgive me for almost taking the mark. When I awoke I was sick all over, to think I might have taken the mark. I asked God what the dream meant. I believe God was telling me to pay closer attention to what is going on around me. I was given this scripture.

> **Be sober, be vigilant; because your adversary the devil, as a roaring lion, walketh about, seeking whom he may devour.**
>
> **1 Peter 5: 8**

People need to be awakened from there slumber. This awful mark is going to happen, just as subtle and unaware to people as in my dream.

There are so many false doctrines and false teachers in this time, if you don't know the true word of God you can be deceived into believing every lie they are telling. As Christians we need to pay very close attention to what is being taught, so we can lead others to the truth, so they will not be lost.

Although I believe the Church will be raptured before the anti-Christ comes on scene, I believe the wheels are now turning to set things into motion for this Biblical prophecy to come to pass. I do not know, nor does anyone else know, when this time of marking will take place. God alone has that answer, but be assured God's word does not lie. He said it will come to pass and it will.

> **And he causeth all, both small and great, rich and poor, free and bond, to receive a mark in their right hand, or on their foreheads;**
>
> **And that no man might buy or sell, save he that had the mark, or the name of the beast, or the number of his name.**
>
> **Here is wisdom. Let him that hath understanding count the number of the beast; for it is the number of a man; and his number is six hundred threescore and six. (666)**
>
> **Matthew 13: 16-18**

For those who do take the mark, the Bible has this to say.

And the third angel followed them, saying with a loud voice, if any man worship the beast and his image and receive his mark in his forehead, or in his hand, the same shall drink of the wine of the wrath of God, which is poured out without mixture into the cup of his indignation; and he shall be tormented with fire and brimstone in the presence of the holy angels, and in the presence of the Lamb;

And the smoke of their torment ascendeth up forever and ever; and they have no rest day nor night, who worship the beast and his image whosoever receiveth the mark of his name.

Revelation 14: 9-11

God does not want anyone to perish, or to go through the great tribulation. There are some people that do not know what the book of Revelation has to say about the anti-Christ. There are others that refuse to believe this man of sin will ever come, but my friend, he is coming! I am giving you the warning, and the chance to repent of your sins, and accept Jesus as you Savior, and be saved and escape the great tribulation. It does not matter if you believe the book of Revelation or not it is still true, and the awful horror of it will happen to all unbelievers. If your heart is stirring in you to repent and be saved it is so easy. Just sincerely pray this prayer:

Jesus, please come into my heart, I believe you are the Son of God, you were born of a virgin, died on the cross for my sins, was buried, and arose on the third day, ascended into haven, and you are sitting at the

right hand of God the Father. I repent of all my sins. Please forgive me. Thank you Jesus, Amen.

Welcome to the family of God!

For God so loved the world, that he gave his only begotten Son, that whosoever believeth in Him shall not perish, but have everlasting life.

John 3: 16

God speaks to me in many different ways. Reading the Bible, through preachers and teachers, He sends people to me, in songs, in my dreams and in visions, in my prayers, a whisper, and a touch. How does God speak to you? Are you listening?

For God speaketh once, yea twice, yet man perceiveth it not.

In a dream, in a vision of the night, when deep sleep falleth upon men, in slumbering upon the bed;

Then He openeth the ears of men, and sealeth their instructions.

Job 33: 14-16

Come unto me, all ye that labour and are heavy laden and I will give you rest.

Take my yoke upon you, and learn of me; for I am meek and lowly in heart; and ye shall find rest unto your souls.

For my yoke is easy, and my burden is light.

Matthew 11: 28-30

✠ ✠ ✠

About the Author

I was born August 27, 1948, to Leo and Peg (Houchin) Miller. The youngest of four children, my brothers were Jim and Chuck. My sister is Merlena. My mother was a God-fearing, God-loving Christian lady and my inspiration.

We grew up in Belle Center, Ohio. I married Doug Collins on October 24, 1965. We have three children: Tonya, Christy, and Eric. Four grandchildren: Seth, Caitlin, Rebecca, and Shelby.

I love my Lord and Saviour Jesus Christ above all else on this earth. My desire is to bring the lost into His Kingdom.

Marieta Miller-Collins